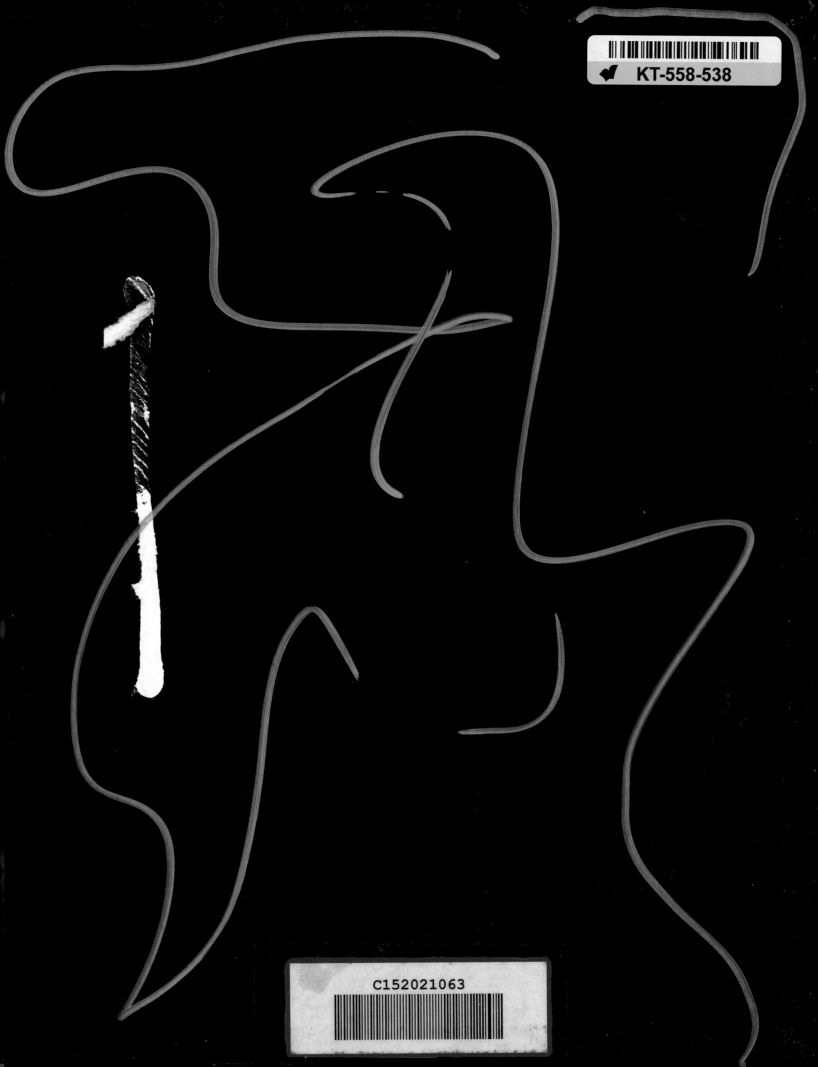

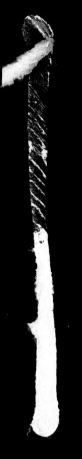

20TH CENTURY fashion

THE 40s & 50s
UTILITY to NEW LOOK

20TH CENTURY FASHION – THE '40s & '50s
was produced by

David West ꙮ Children's Books
7 Princeton Court
55 Felsham Road
London SW15 1AZ

Picture Research: Carlotta Cooper/Brooks Krikler
Research
Editor: Clare Oliver

First published in Great Britain in 1999 by
Heinemann Library, Halley Court, Jordan Hill,
Oxford OX2 8EJ, a division of Reed Educational and
Professional Publishing Limited.

OXFORD MELBOURNE AUCKLAND
JOHANNESBURG BLANTYRE GABORONE
IBADAN PORTSMOUTH (NH) USA CHICAGO

Copyright © 1999 David West Children's Books

01 00
10 9 8 7 6 5 4 3 2

ISBN 0 431 09550 7 (HB)
ISBN 0 431 09557 4 (PB)

British Library Cataloguing in Publication Data

Reynolds, Helen
Utility to new look (1940s - 1950s). - (Fashion in the
twentieth century)
1. Fashion - History - 20th century - Juvenile
literature
2. Costume - 20th century - Juvenile literature
I. Title
391'.00904

Printed and bound in Italy.

PHOTO CREDITS :
Abbreviations: t-top, m-middle,
b-bottom, r-right, l-left
Cover tl, bm & pages 3tl, 10tl,
14tl, 14bm, 17tr, 18br: Vogue
Magazine © Vogue/Condé Nast
Publications Ltd; Cover tr, br &
pages 3br, 12-13, 24bl, 24-25, 25tr,
26tl, 27br, 27bl: Redferns; Cover m
& pages 5tr, 6tl, 6bl, 7tr, 8tl, 8r,
10-11, 11tr, 11bm, 11br, 12bl,
13tl, 13tr, 15tr, 17br, 19tr.1, 19tr.2,
20l, 21tl, 22bl, 25br, 28tr, 28br,
28-29, 29bl: Hulton Getty; Cover
bl & pages 3tr, 9ml, 15tl: Rawlings
©Vogue/Condé Nast Publications
Ltd; 4mr: Henry Clarke ©
Vogue/Condé Nast Publications
Ltd; 5tl, 15b, 21tr, 24tl, 26tr:
Kobal Collection; 5mr, 10bl, 16br,
19br: Cecil Beaton © Vogue/Condé
Nast Publications Ltd; 5bl, 6br,
7bl, 9tr, 12tl, 13br, 21bl, 22-23,
23br, 26bl: Pictorial Press; 9br.1:
Renovations © Vogue/Condé Nast
Publications Ltd; 9br.2: Rene
Bouet-Willeumez © Vogue/Condé
Nast Publications Ltd; 16tl:
Seeberger © Vogue/Condé Nast
Publications Ltd; 16bl, 20r, 23ml,
25l: Corbis; 16-17: Rene Bouche ©
Vogue/Condé Nast Publications
Ltd; 18tl: Carl Erickson ©
Vogue/Condé Nast Publications
Ltd; 18bl: Piguet © Vogue/Condé
Nast Publications Ltd; 18-19:
Blumenfeld © Vogue/Condé Nast
Publications Ltd; 19bl: Coffin ©
Vogue/Condé Nast Publications
Ltd; 23tr: Caradog Williams ©
Vogue/Condé Nast Publications
Ltd; 27tr: Mary Evans Picture
Library; 29tr: Vernier ©
Vogue/Condé Nast Publications.

With special thanks to the Picture
Library & Syndication Department
at Vogue Magazine/Condé Nast
Publications Ltd.

*An explanation of difficult
words can be found in the
glossary on page 30.*

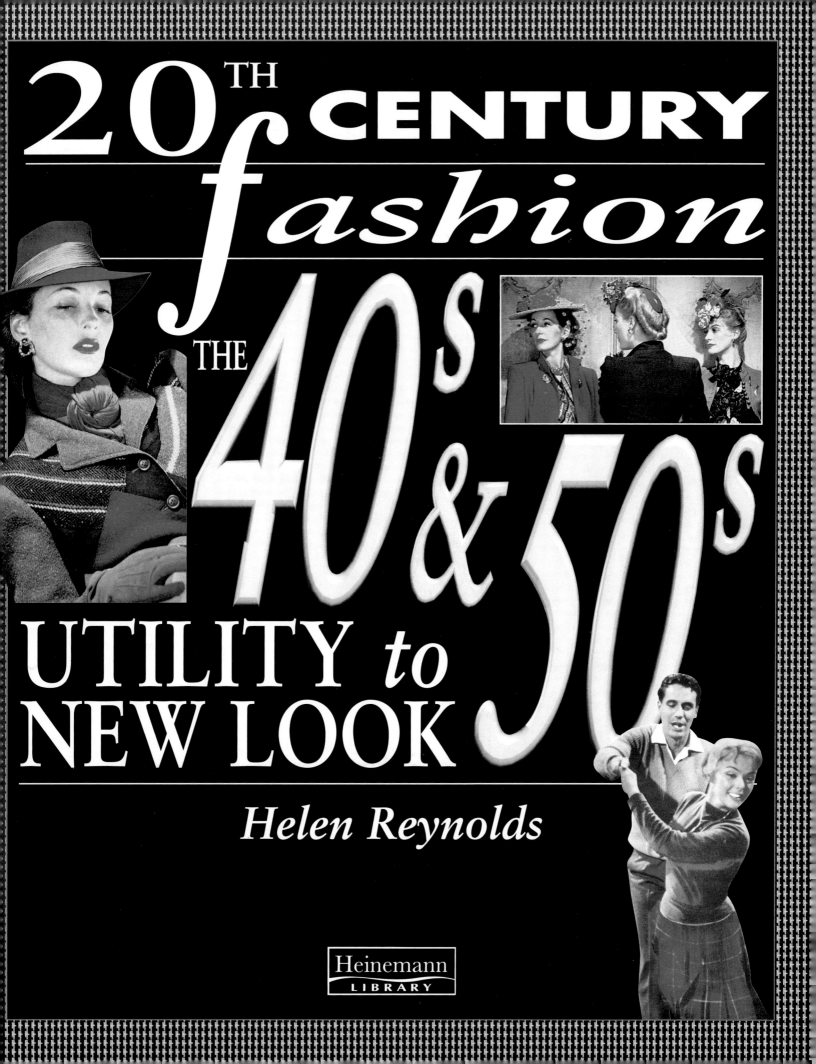

CONTENTS

Chanel reopened her fashion house in '54. This stylish suit ('58) is in easy-to-wear jersey. By the late '50s, women in search of comfort moved away from the constrictions of Dior's New Look.

The United States was the birthplace of youth crazes. At coffee bars and soda fountains, teenagers showed off their newest clothes and danced to the jukebox sounds of the latest pop hits (right).

The hard '40s & the rocking '50s

Momentous changes came during the 1940s and '50s, and most stemmed from the unusual circumstances of World War II. As the men fought, women performed traditionally male jobs, for which they needed practical styles of clothing.

Members of the Women's Auxiliary Air Force (WAAF) load stores on to an RAF truck. From the beginning of the war, women did their bit.

Betty Grable was the queen of the pin-up girls. Her legs were insured for a million dollars!

By necessity, it was accepted that mass-produced clothing could be as fashionable as haute couture. Top magazines, such as *Vogue*, photographed factory-made, ready-to-wear fashion and displayed it alongside couture. Styles during the war were hard-wearing and sensible.

Glamour was confined to the cinema screen and to the pin-up photos that kept up morale amongst the servicemen far from home.

When the war was over, ordinary women reacted against the long years of making do. Christian Dior presented his New Look in February '47. Before long, this feminine silhouette of full skirts, tight waists and sloping shoulders had filtered down into mainstream fashion.

Clothes were rationed so they had to be versatile. This light, woollen dress ('43) could be worn all year round.

Finally, there was a baby boom after the war when husbands and wives were reunited.

By the time of the prosperous '50s, these babies had grown up – into teenagers. These young people eagerly developed their own culture and fashion. Rock 'n' roll was born in '55, and from then on music and youth style would always be closely linked.

The '50s was a time of great excitement. An explosion of new technologies made everything seem possible. By the end of the decade, the silicon chip had been invented and the first satellite had been successfully launched into space. A new age was about to begin.

Fashions of <u>War</u>

When the 1940s dawned, Europe was already three months into a total war: World War II (1939–45). For the first half of the decade, fashion took a back seat as every available person and material was pulled into the war effort.

THE HOME FRONT

At first, only women without family commitments were directed into war work. They worked on farms and in factories, and they nursed in the hospitals that sprang up to serve the fighting services. Soon, nurseries and child-care centres freed more women for essential war work.

Members of the Women's Auxiliary Air Force (WAAF) had to learn new skills. Practicality was more important than femininity.

JOINING UP

Women were quickly encouraged to help the war effort more directly. Whether they joined land, sea or air forces and whether they were on the side of the allies or the axis powers of Germany, Italy and, later, Japan, military women were all issued with a hardwearing uniform. Uniform colours were chosen to provide camouflage in the field, so they tended to be drab and practical.

Tropical uniform for Wrens (Women's Royal Naval Service) came in cool, light-coloured cotton.

A German *Stabshelferin* wore field grey, while a US servicewoman might wear brown. Usually, women's uniforms featured a skirt rather than trousers. Otherwise, women dressed in similar fashion to military men. Shoes were flat and built for comfort, while buttoned pockets provided storage space for vital papers or equipment. Badges stitched on to the lapels, shoulders or sleeves indicated the servicewoman's rank.

DESIGNERS DO THEIR BIT

Fashion designers were pulled in to design the uniforms. Having closed his Parisian salon, Chicago-born Mainbocher (1891–1976) returned to the United States where he designed part of the Women's Red Cross uniform. In Britain, Irish designer Digby Morton (1906–83) designed new uniforms for the Women's Voluntary Service (WVS).

Pilots no longer wore fancy braided uniforms, but bomber jackets.

BOMBER JACKETS
Known in the UK as bomber jackets, and in the US as battle jackets, these warm, military-issue short jackets were made of thick leather or wool. In the '50s, they became popular with youths – today, they are worn by young and old alike.

The US marines' cap could be worn in two different ways. Even in uniform, women tried to create their own unique look.

ON CIVVY STREET

Not surprisingly, civilian clothes took on a military air. Designers used uniforms as a source of inspiration and classic, tailored suits were popular. Although the lines changed little from the late 1930s, skirts became shorter, shoulders squarer, trousers leaner and shoes sturdier. For practical reasons, many more women started to wear trousers. By '45, the silhouette had softened a little, but in general fashion did not change much during the war. This was because there were not enough resources for people to buy new items each season. Instead, they bought clothes only when their old ones had worn out.

RATIONING & *making do*

During World War II, merchant navy ships carrying materials or clothes were often sunk by enemy submarines. In addition, clothing manufacturers were concentrating on making uniforms rather than civilian clothes.

A customer buying groceries had to hand over her ration-book. Rationing stopped people buying more than their fair share of goods.

NOT ENOUGH TO GO ROUND

There was also a shortage of labour. People who had worked as tailors and dressmakers, or in textile and clothing factories, were now in better-paid war-related work. At first, there were stocks of clothes that had been made before the war. As these ran out, governments were forced to act.

FAIR SHARE FOR ALL

In Britain, rationing was introduced on 1 June 1941 and continued until March '49. During World War I, high prices had stopped people buying too much. This meant that poorer families simply could not afford to buy enough food and clothing. In World War II, the government wanted to ensure that, regardless of income, everyone had a 'fair share' of the limited resources.

In the '40s, it was the fashion to wear seamed stockings. But nylons were hard to come by. Some women made do with drawn-on seams and bare legs!

COUPONS FOR CLOTHES

Everyone was given a ration-book full of coupons. At first every person had 66 coupons per year. This was later reduced, as shortages intensified. Shops had to take the right number of coupons from a customer as well as the correct money. Whatever the price, similar items had the same coupon value. For example, any man's jacket was valued at 26 coupons, a blouse at 12 coupons and a pair of men's shoes at 18 coupons. When the coupons ran out, no more clothes could be bought until the next ration-book was issued.

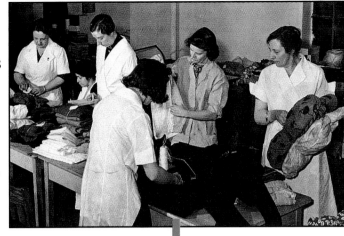

American charities collected second-hand clothes to send in parcels to the people in war-torn Europe.

THRIFTY SHOPPERS

Rationing made impulse buying a thing of the past. People thought hard about what they bought, fearful they might run out of essential items, such as shoes. Most people used all their coupons. However some people did sell coupons for cash, or persuaded friends in ration-free countries to send them clothes. And although rationing stopped wealthy people getting all the clothes, it did not stop manufacturers using scarce fabric in clothes that only the rich could afford.

For the first time, people were urged to mix and match colours to make the best use of scarce material.

MAKING NEW FROM OLD

Of course, unless a home – and the wardrobe inside it – was destroyed in an air raid, people had clothes from before the war. In June '43 *Vogue* featured a print by the American designer Count René Willaumez. It looked as if it was made up of scarfs – readers were encouraged to copy the effect by seaming together real scarfs. The magazine had also provided patterns for ten different items of clothing that could be made from a pre-war evening dress!

Magazines were filled with bright ideas for giving old, tired clothes items a new lease of life.

UTILITY *fashion*

Rationing alone was not enough to ensure that clothing was fairly priced and that manufacturers were not wasteful with cloth such as silk (which was needed for parachutes). In Britain, these problems were addressed by the Utility Scheme, while in the United States the L85 laws imposed limits on the use of silk and wool.

Unheard of before the '40s, a Vogue cover ('41) featured a trouser suit.

STEPS TO UTILITY

Top British designers worked on the Utility range, including Hardy Amies, Norman Hartnell (who later designed the Queen's wedding dress), Edward Molyneux, Digby Morton, Victor Stiebel and Bianca Mosca. The plan was to design a practical, durable wardrobe of a coat, a suit, a shirt or blouse and a dress.

RULES & REGULATIONS

The Utility scheme controlled the price and quality of 85% of all cloth manufactured. Clothes had to conform to strict regulations – a dress could not have more than two pockets or five buttons. The number of seams, pleats and the length of stitching were controlled. Designs could be rejected if they were not 'austere' enough: a Molyneux suit, for example, was rejected because of its wasteful turned-back cuffs and lavish pocket flaps!

Non-Utility designers created hard-wearing clothes, too. In '43 Jaeger presented this suit of green tweed and striped flannel.

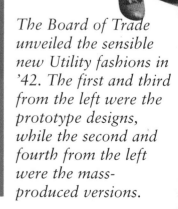

The Board of Trade unveiled the sensible new Utility fashions in '42. The first and third from the left were the prototype designs, while the second and fourth from the left were the mass-produced versions.

INTO PRODUCTION

Once the designs had been chosen, manufacturers were given licences to mass-produce the clothing. The government made sure the licence-holders received the bulk of the raw materials that could be spared for civilian use. In return, the manufacturers promised to follow the Utility patterns to the letter and had to obey the strict guidelines on quantity and price. At first they had misgivings about the scheme, but they soon supported it – because all the clothes they produced sold out, they never had surplus 'sale' stock.

Utility schemes controlled furniture manufacture too.

UTILITY IN THE HOME

Homes were not only furnished with Utility. The pottery firm Wedgwood did its bit, bringing out a line of crockery designed for 'simplicity of manufacture and minimum breakage': Victory Ware!

UTILITY FOR ALL

Utility clothes quickly gained a reputation for endurance. The scheme continued after the war up until 1952, long after rationing had stopped. Not all clothes produced at the time were Utility. But even non-Utility hand-tailored clothes were sometimes made from the hard-wearing Utility fabrics.

Utility clothes were designed to survive the toughest jobs as women took to wielding tools, from pitchforks to blowlamps.

DANCING *the* night away

The war made people more determined than ever to have a good time. Death was so commonplace that people wanted to 'live for today'. Whether they had been working all week in a munitions factory or were finally home on leave, people wanted to go out and dance their cares away. Lacking eveningwear, civilians put on their tidiest clothes, while servicemen and women wore uniform.

Glenn Miller (1904–44) was the biggest musical star of the war years.

GLENN MILLER
Miller led a string of popular orchestras and was known for his 'sweet' sound. His hits included *Moonlight Serenade*, *Little Brown Jug* and *In the Mood*. He joined up in '42, forming the Glenn Miller Air Force Band to entertain the troops. He died in '44, when his plane was shot down in the English Channel.

AMERICA TAKES THE LEAD
Swing was the big thing. Glenn Miller, Benny Goodman, Artie Shaw and other star bandleaders sold millions of records. For slower dances, there were numbers by crooners such as Bing Crosby, or sentimental tear-jerkers by Vera Lynn.

British women were bussed to dances to partner US soldiers. Most women owned only one pair of shoes and these were practical rather than elegant.

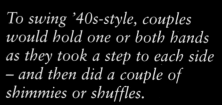

To swing '40s-style, couples would hold one or both hands as they took a step to each side – and then did a couple of shimmies or shuffles.

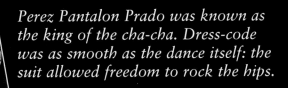

Perez Pantalon Prado was known as the king of the cha-cha. Dress-code was as smooth as the dance itself: the suit allowed freedom to rock the hips.

JITTERBUGGING GIs

The young, too, took their cue from the United States. US soldiers, nicknamed GIs, short for government issue, brought lavish supplies of nylons to Europe – they also brought over the jitterbug, or jive. Performed to pacey jazz, this was a fast, jerky dance in which the female partner was thrown acrobatically around!

Parisian students jitterbugged too in '49. But the look was different – baseball boots gave great grip.

LATIN LOVERS

By the early 1950s the cha-cha was all the rage. Invented by the Cuban bandleader Enrique Jorrín, this fast dance was similar to the mambo. Looking to Latin America, which had been untouched by the war, was a form of escapism. Clothes too had a holiday feel, with off-the-shoulder dresses for women and loose-fitting suits for the men.

By the late '50s, everyone was jiving. In summer '57, there was a dance 'marathon', when over 2,000 youngsters on board a boat jived their way across the English Channel.

HOLLYWOOD *glamour*

Many of the wartime jobs that women did involved hard work in dirty conditions. So they wore unflattering jodhpurs and dungarees or adapted men's overalls. For safety, they tied back their hair or wrapped it up in a turban. After the initial excitement at wearing workmen's clothes, many longed for a Ginger Roger's gown or flowing, wavy hair as worn by Veronica Lake. Such luxuries were impractical – and some impossible to come by – but they could be admired from afar on the silver screen.

Wearing a rich sheepskin coat, this Vogue *cover girl of '43 was the cheering epitome of Hollywood chic. The number of buttons on her waistcoat was very extravagant for the time!*

MORALE-BOOSTING MOVIES

Although cinema did offer news and information, most movie-goers sought entertainment and escapism. Women in particular wanted to soak up the extravagant elegance of the stars. They were not disappointed. Governments understood that the cinema was an important way for people to take their minds off the war. Film companies were allowed to buy some of the limited luxury cloth available, and make it into styles for their film stars that flouted austerity regulations.

This feminine trilby appeared in a Vogue *magazine in '43 and later became popularised in the classic movie,* Brief Encounter *('45).*

SCREEN ROMANCE

Romantic films were the best form of escapism. Classics such as *Casablanca* ('42) were shot in moody black and white.

Magazine readers were urged to recreate inexpensively the film-star feel of these New York suits ('42) by wearing real flowers as accessories.

Bette Davis and Joan Crawford were smoulderingly sophisticated; musicals such as *Cover Girl*, starring Rita Hayworth, featured more frivolous fashions.

HOME-SPUN GLAMOUR
Magazines tried to convey the drama of Hollywood on their pages. They suggested ways in which plain clothes could be dressed up. Make-up was another way for a woman to grab a little slice of glamour – make-up was available in the shops and magazines featured eye-catching advertisements and tips on how to apply it. Women copied their film-star heroines' techniques.

Despite Casablanca's *war-time setting, its stars Ingrid Bergman and Humphrey Bogart oozed glamour.*

PARIS *fights back*

Pre-war Paris had been considered the capital of the fashion world. Then, in summer 1940, the city was occupied by German soldiers. Paris was suddenly cut off from the rest of the world.

After Paris was liberated, French designers put on a travelling Théâtre de la Mode *(fashion show) to promote Parisian couture.*

BEHIND THE LINES

Those designers who were not French, such as Charles Creed, Mainbocher, Edward Molyneux and Elsa Schiaparelli, closed down and left France. French-born Coco Chanel closed too, but stayed in Paris. Jacques Heim, who was Jewish, went into hiding. However, over 90 couture houses stayed open. Designers Pierre Balmain, Christian Dior, Lucien Lelong and Nina Ricci all continued to work in Nazi-occupied Paris. Having lost their British and American clientele, they sold to the wives and mistresses of Nazi officers.

Parisian streets and cafés were crowded with German soldiers on Bastille Day, July '40. Paris was occupied for four years.

This Schiaparelli outfit featured in her '45 collection. The scarf was a patriotic design in red, white and blue.

For the collections of '45 many designers, such as Schiaparelli, returned to Paris. This outfit from her show had a high beaver-felt hat and chin-hugging scarf. Such items were described as 'Directoire' because they harked back to the styles popular when France was at the height of its power, in the Directorate period (1795–99).

LIBERTÉ!

After Paris was freed in August 1944, American *Vogue* did a feature on Paris fashions. While British and American designers had simplified their clothes, Paris couturiers had continued in their pre-war, opulent style. *Vogue*'s editor, Edna Woolman Chase, said that the French designers had been patriotic by wasting Nazi labour and materials. Even so, many wealthy European women shunned Parisian couture.

VOGUE
INCLUDING VOGUE PATTERN BOOK
Spring Fabrics and Renovation
MARCH, 1945
PRICE 3/-

The French look included costly furs and a lavish use of silks for gloves and headgear.

A TRAVELLING FASHION SHOW

To fire up interest, designers in Paris created a *Théâtre de la Mode*, a travelling exhibition of tiny mannequins that displayed the garments in miniature. This show, which started in Paris, and then toured America and Europe, was a huge success. It put Parisian couture back on the map … but it would take Dior's 'New Look' to tempt back the international clients.

THE DE-MOB SUIT

At the end of the war, people leaving the armed forces had few civilian clothes. In Britain, a demobilization clothing programme was set up. Ex-servicewomen received a cash allowance and clothing coupons, but men were given a 'de-mob' outfit consisting of a suit, an overcoat, a shirt with two detachable collars, a tie, two pairs of socks, a pair of shoes and a hat. Some men wore their de-mob clothes well into the '50s, unable to buy replacements.

De-mob clothes were mass-produced to Utility specifications – they were robust but not stylish.

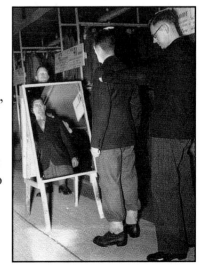

DIOR & the New Look

Despite the initial outrage at the extravagance of wartime French couture, by 1947 women everywhere were tired of 'practical' fashion. Sensing the mood, Christian Dior set up his own fashion house backed by the textile industrialist Marcel Boussac.

This Dior design of '47 creates the classic New Look silhouette. A wool coat reveals flowing taffeta pleats.

Few could afford the mink collar but Dior's romantic and feminine New Look shape was loved and copied by many.

FEMININITY IN FASHION

On 12 February 1947, Dior unveiled his New Look. Its essence was its sloping shoulders, tight bodice, hand-span waist and full billowing skirts, which fell to mid-calf. This created a feminine, hour-glass figure which was set off with simple jewellery, silk stockings and stiletto-heeled shoes. Other essential accessories included a hat, often worn to one side, and long gloves. It marked a return to elegance – and women adored it.

This outfit from Piguet, March '47, had a 'top-heavy' look, from its huge hat and big collar to the tiny, pinched waist.

To achieve the perfect figure, women wore lace-up corsets, or bras and girdles. Some underwear was boned, some used strong supportive elastics, such as Lastex.

LAVISH … OR WASTEFUL?

Dior had set out to 'liberate all women from a poverty-stricken era'. Including petticoats, each New Look outfit required up to 45 metres of fabric – by comparison, less than three metres had gone into a typical British wartime dress. Even though the war was over, British women could only marvel at the New Look, since rationing was still part of their lives. The Junior Trade Minister said the new fashion was 'irresponsibly frivolous and wasteful'. But as the austerity regulations were lifted, the New Look was adapted for mass-manufacture, and a straight-skirted alternative was introduced.

FOUNDATIONS FOR FASHION

To achieve the New Look silhouette, women had to be as extravagant with their underwear as with their outerwear. Dior stated firmly that 'Without foundations, there can be no fashion'. Ample petticoats created the full skirt, but this had to be accentuated with a tiny waist.

CORSET CONTROL

Corsets came back into fashion. A new version called the waspie, or waist cincher, had been introduced by Marcel Rochas in 1946. It covered only the waist, but was still extremely uncomfortable: whalebone was used to achieve the shape. Before long, roll-ons were used instead, which used clever stitching to hold the figure firmly in place.

This Molyneux dress of '47 featured tiered three-quarter length sleeves, rounded shoulders and a soft sash draping from the hip.

THE BIKINI AND THE BOMB

Not all fashions coming from Paris used lots of material. In '46, a designer called Louis Réard created a skimpy two-piece swimsuit. At the same time, couturier Jacques Heim created one too, which he christened the *atome*. On 1 July that year, the United States conducted its first atomic test on the Bikini Atoll in the Pacific and tore the island in two. The *atome* soon became the bikini.

A contestant for France's 'Most Beautiful Bather of '46' modelled the new bikini.

Sloping shoulders were not new. Molyneux had used them in '41 with the loose raglan sleeves of this flowing yellow coat.

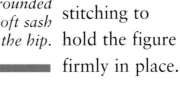

REBELS *without a cause*

The drape jackets and drainpipe trousers of the teddy boys were supposed to be a revival of men's dress during the reign of King Edward VII. A first step towards a classless society, the 'yobs' were imitating the 'nobs'.

After the hard years of the 1940s, the '50s heralded affluence, disposable income and confidence. A baby boom (as servicemen returned home from the war and started to have families) swelled the teenage population from the mid-'50s. There was plenty of work to go round and, as most youngsters lived at home, they suddenly had more spending power than ever before.

Marlon Brando appeared as a drag-racing teenage rebel in The Wild One *('54).*

FASHION STATEMENT

As young people became better educated, they developed a political and social conscience. Working-class youths in Britain expressed their views on social injustice by adopting the Saville Row dress of upper-class 'nobs' for themselves. These teddy boys strutted around in brothelcreepers and tailored suits.

JUVENILE DELINQUENTS

Between 1956 and '61, eight movies had titles that included the word 'teenager.' Still more took restless youth as their subject. *Lost, Lonely and Vicious* ('58) showed American teenagers racing about in cars, hanging out and experimenting with sex.

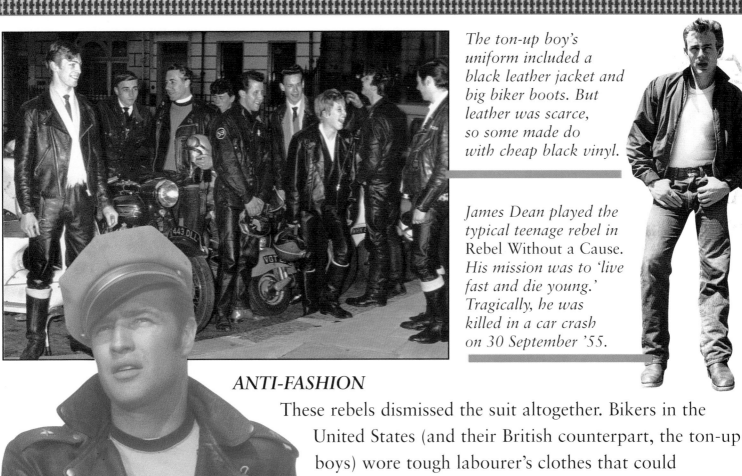

The ton-up boy's uniform included a black leather jacket and big biker boots. But leather was scarce, so some made do with cheap black vinyl.

James Dean played the typical teenage rebel in Rebel Without a Cause. *His mission was to 'live fast and die young.' Tragically, he was killed in a car crash on 30 September '55.*

ANTI-FASHION

These rebels dismissed the suit altogether. Bikers in the United States (and their British counterpart, the ton-up boys) wore tough labourer's clothes that could withstand the time spent on the seat of a motorbike. The items that were to prove most popular and enduring were leather jackets, jeans and teeshirts, as worn by screen rebels and idols, such as Marlon Brando and James Dean.

THE FIRST LEVI'S

Jeans were first introduced to the United States as workwear in the 1850s by Levi Strauss. He sold his dyed-denim trousers to the gold-rushers. Today, of course, they are worn by just about everyone – not just teenage rebels.

Teeshirts were first worn by US soldiers, then by workmen. They were adopted by rebellious youths during the '50s.

AMERICA & consumerism

With Paris closed during the war, American designers could no longer seek inspiration from the twice-yearly French shows. Instead, they started to make their own casual clothes and sportswear. These styles were ideal for women's increasingly active roles. And they could be easily mass-produced in huge quantities.

Post-war America idealised the model nuclear family. Most women were homemakers, keeping their children, their home and themselves neat and tidy.

THE ALL-AMERICAN FAMILY

After the war, new technologies such as fridges, television sets, washing machines and cars became available to almost every middle-class family in America. In theory, this freed up women to spend more time on looking good, as the brand-new consumer goods took care of the day-to-day drudgery. Doris Day portrayed the new female role in her films, playing the model wife – who wears co-ordinating pastel separates.

The comfortable twinset always looked good. Pastel shades were considered most feminine. A neat boxy handbag completed the look.

PRACTICAL DAYWEAR

The United States had always been at the forefront of producing practical womenswear. In the 1850s, Amelia Bloomer (1818–94) had pioneered Turkish-style trousers for women.

The most-influential American fashion designer of the 1950s was Claire McCardell (1905–58). Her clothes were sporty, relaxed, comfortable and functional. She worked in simple fabrics, such as cotton, jersey, denim and chambray. Neat gingham checks were a popular pattern. Other hallmarks were the wraparound dress and the softly-pleated full dirndl skirt. The emphasis was on health, fitness and sport.

Paris took note. With his bonbonnière collection ('58), shoemaker Charles Jourdan celebrated the candybox palette so popular in the US: pineapple yellow, cherry pink and clear glacier blue.

McCardell's swimwear used soft fabrics and a natural shape.

COMFORT AT LAST
Starting work in the late '20s, Claire McCardell developed what became known as the American Look. McCardell designed practical, comfortable clothes for active women, taking simple shapes and superimposing them with pockets, contrasting topstitching, hooks and rivets.

MIX & MATCH SEPARATES
Another American designer who pioneered functional clothes was Bonnie Cashin (b.1915). She worked in leather, canvas, poplin, suede and tweed and created easy-to-wear kimonos, tabards, ponchos, hooded coats and long, mohair-fringed skirts. These layered clothes were the exact opposite of Dior's carefully assembled New Look. Instead, a woman's wardrobe consisted of a number of brightly-coloured separates that were mixed and matched to create a variety of comfortable outfits suitable for any occasion.

COMPLETING THE LOOK
This casual style of dressing meant that, before long, the hat fell from favour. Cosmetics, on the other hand, became more popular than ever. Everyone had to have firmly pencilled eyebrows, mascara-laden lashes and luscious glossy lips.

The tight-fitting sweater was worn with a sculpted bra. Actress and pin-up Jayne Mansfield had the classic 'missile' silhouette!

ZOOTIES, HIPSTERS & BEATNIKS

There were two basic trends in underground fashion of the period – dressing up and dressing down. As a rule, underground chic aimed to escape the class one started out in.

Jazz musician Cab Calloway wears an over-sized zoot suit in the slick all-black movie Stormy Weather *('43).*

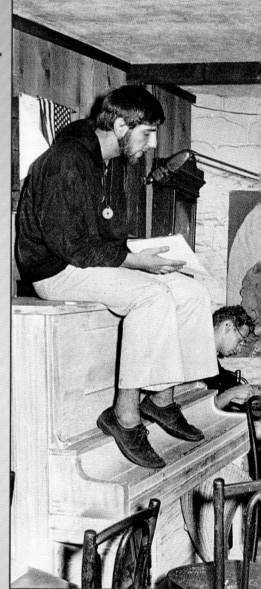

BIRTH OF THE ZOOT SUIT

Long before the modernists emerged in the late '40s, a flamboyant suit-wearing style had grown out of the streets of Harlem, New York. Under-privileged blacks and Mexicans who had 'made good' dressed up in baggy suits that came in a rainbow of peacock colours. The zoot suit became the uniform of all the top jazz stars of the day. However, the zooties were criticised during the war, when clothing restrictions came in.

Public outcry at such wastage led to the 'zoot suit riots' that began in Los Angeles in '43, when white servicemen attacked and stripped some Mexican-American zooties, and soon spread to other major US cities. The French had their own zootie style, known as *zazou*. They too openly ignored the restrictions on clothing imposed by the German occupiers and suffered similar attacks.

Thelonius Monk's baggy-suited jazz band, photographed in the '50s outside Minton's Playhouse, Harlem, the birthplace of bebop.

GROOVY HIPSTERS

Following the war, a new form of jazz called bebop became popular. More experimental than the swing of the zooties, bebop stars included Thelonius Monk and Charlie Parker.

Suits slimmed down from the zoot, but were still baggy and in wilder fabrics. Dizzy Gillespie's leopardskin jacket was legendary. Berets were popular headgear and shades were a must. Hipsters had their own sound, look and slang: clothes, for example, were called 'threads.'

Machito's rhythm section wear 'Cool School' collarless jackets. By the late '40s, jazz had become associated with the sleek modernist look.

THE BEAT GENERATION

The hipsters were not the only ones to 'dig' jazz. The beatniks loved jazz and its counterpart, poetry. It was a tradition begun in Paris by Jean-Paul Sartre. Now the leading lights were the author, Jack Kerouac and the poet, Alan Ginsberg (who later coined the term 'flower power'). Bohemian fashion involved dressing down and black was a favourite colour. Women wore men's shirts over tight pedal-pushers or trousers. Haircuts were short. By the end of the 1950s, the bohemian look had reached Hollywood, most notably in *Breakfast at Tiffany's* ('61), starring the elfin-faced Audrey Hepburn.

Beatniks would hold poetry readings. New York's Greenwich Village was the capital of the beatnik scene, but bohemian Paris was its inspiration.

French model Capucine wore beatnik pedal-pushers with an outsize shirt ('58). 'Must-have' footwear was wedged heels and ballet straps.

MALCOLM X
Fashion can make powerful political statements. The zoot suits of the early '40s were one of the earliest expressions of black pride, so it is not surprising that Malcolm X (1925–65) was, in his time, a zootie, a hipster and, finally, a modernist.

Black civil rights activist Malcolm X was shot dead at a rally in '65.

ROCK 'N' ROLL
& the new youth culture

Bill Haley and the Comets' Rock Around the Clock ('55) marked the birth of rock 'n' roll.

The summer of 1955 witnessed the birth of a momentous new musical style. Rock 'n' roll had arrived. Originating in the United States, it fused the sounds of country and western with rhythm and blues. To go with this wild new music would come wild new looks for its young fans.

Elvis was famous for his two-tone shoes as well as for the way he wriggled his hips in his snug jeans.

SODA-FOUNTAIN STYLE

Teenage fans of the new rock 'n' roll wore clothes to show off on the dance floor. Full, knee-length skirts with tight elasticated belts were worn over layers upon layers of nylon net petticoats. More often than not, these skirts sported checks or large polka-dots. Bobbysocks and flat shoes finished the outfit and girls wore their hair tied up in a ponytail which would flick from side to side as they danced the energetic new steps.

JUKEBOX JURY

The meeting place for British teenagers was the coffee bar and, in the United States, the soda fountain (a bar selling soft drinks called sodas). In pride of place, a jukebox played all the latest tunes.

Teenagers chose their favourite records on the jukebox.

ROCKABILLY KING

Meanwhile, Elvis Presley was performing to hoardes of screaming teenage fans. His southern rock 'n' roll style later came to be known as rockabilly. Rockabilly was unusual in that it embraced two opposite styles of dress – hipster and biker. Elvis might appear in a dandy suit and two-tone shoes one day, then in torn jeans and a teeshirt the next. Rockabilly boys favoured suits in pastel shades. Underneath, a patterned shirt with outsize collars might be worn. Rockabilly girls, too, were as at home in their denims as in a neat suit.

They wore stylish accessories such as patterned silk scarfs and designer sunglasses.

Rockabilly boys wore their hair slicked back. Girls tied theirs back with ribbons. Clean-cut rockabillies made a come-back in the late-'70s.

INTO THE SWINGING '60s

As the '50s drew to a close, it became clear that fashion would continue to spin off in every direction and that this would be particularly true for youth styles. The teenager was an individual in his or her own right and not someone who copied the styles of their parents. This was going to lead to some outrageous outfits, worn to shock the older generation. And, with pop music central to this new youth culture, in future the concert stage would be as important to fashion as the catwalk.

Flared skirts were worn with tight-fitting sweaters. This showed off the figure, but allowed freedom of movement.

At the soda fountain, youngsters would buy soft drinks and dance to the latest rock 'n' roll.

The TECHNOLOGY *behind the*

In 1939, most clothes were still made individually in small workshops. Each garment was assembled by one worker, much as the couturier does today. This method produced unique garments, but it was not very efficient.

Nylon 'chips'

Hopper

FASHION IN BULK

Mass-production methods had been developed before World War II and were already in use by many big clothing firms. Wartime governments wanted a far higher percentage of clothes to be made in this way, to ensure that scarce materials and precious manpower were used as efficiently as possible. For example, the British Board of Trade issued the majority of its Utility licences to firms who would mass-produce.

Nylons kept their shape. This was achieved by easing them on to metal moulds, then subjecting them to very hot steam.

Nylon chips are heated to make a viscous fluid

Cold air hardens the nylon thread

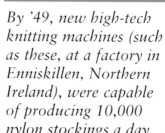

Nylon is forced through spinneret

THE FIRST SYNTHETIC

The fabric of the age was nylon, the first-ever synthetic fabric. Patented in 1937, it went into production at Du Pont's New Jersey plant in '38, where it was first used for toothbrush bristles.

Hot steam 'sets' or fixes the thread

Nylon filaments are twisted into yarn and rolled on to a bobbin

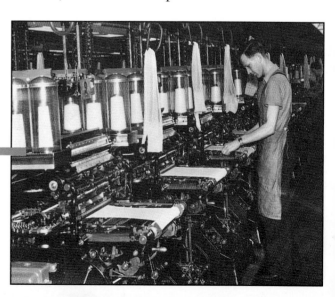

By '49, new high-tech knitting machines (such as these, at a factory in Enniskillen, Northern Ireland), were capable of producing 10,000 nylon stockings a day.

fashions of the '40s & '50s

Nylon could be spun to a much finer gauge than silk. Spinning the finest silk required at least 540 needles, whereas this machine for spinning nylon needed only 400.

In '39, the company started spinning nylon yarn for stockings. The first 'nylons' went on sale in the United States in May '40 – all four million pairs sold out in four days.

Nylon transformed the textile industry. It was easy to dye and its colour did not fade. Unlike silk, it did not wrinkle or 'bag', and did not attract moths.

SUPERFABRIC!

From 1941 (when the United States entered the war) until '45, hardly any stockings were made. The first British-made nylons went on sale in '46. Soon, versatile nylon was being mixed with other natural fibres and used for all sorts of fashion: dresses, blouses, suits, ties and supportive underwear. Du Pont continued to experiment with its new textile, most notably creating a fireproof nylon called aramid in the late '50s that would be used to clothe firefighters and racing drivers.

This Caprice bra ('55) used nylon taffeta for the cups and nylon lace for the trim. The elastic net girdle controlled the body for a sleek silhouette, while its suspender straps held up the nylon stockings.

The fashion for a feminine figure led to some odd inventions! The nylon-rayon inflatable bra appeared in '52. Each cup contained a plastic bubble that was blown up like a balloon to create the perfect bust 'size.

GLOSSARY

BROTHELCREEPER A thick-soled shoe worn by teddy boys.

CHAMBRAY A fabric with a tiny check or mottled effect.

DIRNDL A very full skirt, loosely gathered into soft pleats at the waistband.

DRAINPIPE TROUSERS Trousers with very tight, narrow legs.

DRAPE JACKET A long-line jacket, with velvet-trimmed collar, cuffs and pockets, worn by teddy boys

FILAMENT A fine thread or fibre.

GIRDLE A waist-to-thigh-length corset.

MASS-PRODUCTION Making goods in great quantities, usually through the use of machines.

MODERNIST STYLE A sleek, sharp look popular in the 1950s. Men wore slim, single-breasted suits (sometimes collarless), button-down shirts and narrow, squared-off ties.

PEDAL-PUSHERS Calf-length trousers.

PONCHO A blanket-like cloak.

RAGLAN A sleeve that is sewn in along two diagonal seams from neck to armpit.

ROLL-ON A tightly elasticated, suspenderless corset.

SAVILLE ROW A street in London famous for its tailors.

SPINNERET A small tube through which silk is produced.

STILETTO HEEL A high, narrow shoe heel.

SWING A smooth, orchestral type of jazz popular from the 1930s onwards.

TABARD A hip-length, sleeveless, rectangular top, with a hole for the head to go through.

TAFFETA A shiny, stiff cloth woven from silk or artificial fibres such as rayon.

TON-UP Slang meaning going faster than 100 mph (160kph) on a motorbike.

VISCOUS Of a thick and sticky consistency.

WASPIE A short corset made from whalebone and elasticized fabric, which is laced to draw in the waist.

FASHION HIGHLIGHTS

- USA: first nylon stockings on sale
- Utility Scheme begins
- US Navy issue 'T' shirt
- Zoot suit riots begin
- Cashin in Hollywood
- McCardell designs pump shoes
- Théâtre de la Mode tours USA & Europe
- Rochas: waspie
- First bikinis
- Dior unveils New Look
- Schiaparelli opens house in NY
- Balmain opens ready-to-wear branches in USA
- Utility Scheme ends
- Hartnell: Elizabeth II's coronation gown
- Chanel re-opens her Paris Fashion house
- Mary Quant opens Bazaar
- Balenciaga designs loose 'sack' dress
- Vogue editor, Edna Chase Woolman, dies
- School of Fashion, RCA
- Claire McCardell dies
- Lycra trademarked by Du Pont

TIMELINE

	WORLD EVENTS	TECHNOLOGY	FAMOUS PEOPLE	ART & MEDIA
0	•*World War II continues (1939–45)*		•*McDonald brothers set up first hamburger stand*	•*Stravinsky:* Symphony in C major
1	•*Japanese attack Pearl Harbor; USA enters war*	•*First aerosol spray cans* •*Terylene invented*	•*Death of James Joyce*	•*Brecht:* Mother Courage •*Coward:* Blithe Spirit
2	•*Oxfam founded*	•*First nuclear reactor built in USA*	•*Gandhi imprisoned by British in India*	•*Bergman & Bogart star in* Casablanca
3	•*Mussolini arrested*			•*Sartre:* Being and Nothingness
4	•*Allies land in France & drive back Germans*		•*Glenn Miller killed in plane crash*	•*Henry Moore:* Mother and Child
5	•*Germany & Japan surrender; war ends*	•*First atomic bombs* •*Microwave oven patented*	•*Suicide of Hitler* •*Truman becomes US President*	•*Britten:* Peter Grimes •*Steinbeck:* Cannery Row
6	•*UN General Assembly holds first meetings*	•*First universal electronic computer, ENIAC, built*		•*Picasso:* Reclining Nude •*O'Neill:* The Iceman Cometh
7	•*India & Pakistan gain independence*	•*Sound barrier broken by Yeager in US Bell X-1*	•*Nehru becomes India's first prime minister*	•*Cannes Film Festival opens* •*Camus:* The Plague
8	•*S. Africa: apartheid begins* •*Israel proclaimed*	•*Transistor invented* •*Frisbee patented*	•*Gandhi assassinated*	•*Huston:* Key Largo •*John Wayne in* Red River
9	•*NATO set up* •*East & West Germany formed*		•*Mao proclaims Chinese People's Republic*	•*Eames house completed* •*Orwell:* 1984
0	•*Korean War begins* •*China invades Tibet*	•*First credit card co., Diners Club, founded*	•*McCarthyism begins in USA*	•*Jackson Pollock:* Autumn Rhythm
1		•*First video recording demonstrated*		•*Festival of Britain* •*The African Queen*
2	•*Kenya: Mau Mau revolt begins*		•*Elizabeth II proclaimed Queen on father's death*	•*Le Corbusier:* Unité d'Habitation
3	•*Korea War ends* •*Egypt: Nasser in power*	•*Crick & Watson describe DNA structure*	•*Tensing Norgay & Hillary climb Mt Everest*	•*Osborne:* Look Back in Anger •*Miller:* The Crucible
4	•*SEATO formed*	•*Trials of contraceptive pill start*	•*Roger Bannister runs four-minute mile*	•*Kingsley Amis:* Lucky Jim •*Brando in* The Wild One
5	•*Warsaw Pact formed* •*S. Africa leaves UN*	•*Hovercraft patented* •*Optical fibres patented*	•*Einstein dies* •*James Dean killed in car crash*	•*Patrick White:* Tree of Man •*Hitchcock:* Rear Window
6	•*Suez crisis in Middle East*		•*Elvis Presley's* Heartbreak Hotel *tops US record charts*	•*Beckett:* Waiting for Godot
7	•*EEC (Common Market) founded*	•*USSR launches first satellite, Sputnik 1*	•*Macmillan succeeds Eden as British prime minister*	•*Chagall:* The Circus Rider •*Kerouac:* On the Road
8	•*CND start anti-bomb protests*	•*Heart pacemaker invented* •*First hula-hoop*	•*De Gaulle elected president of France*	•*Chevalier & Caron star in* Gigi
9	•*Cuba: Castro in power* •*US troops sent to Laos*	•*Silicon chips first made* •*Austin mini launched*	•*Buddy Holly dies in plane crash*	•*Mies van der Rohe:* Seagram Building

INDEX